Reflections & Prayers

Scriptures Used In Our Books
With Room for Your Thoughts

We put together this small prayer journal for you.

This is some of our favorite scriptures which we used in our various books by Ruth Price, Rebecca Price and Rachel Stoltzfus.

They are collected here for your enjoyment and reflection. We will add to these as time goes on, and we will compile and send them to you for free as a thanks for reading our books.

We have left lots of room for you to write your thoughts and reflections. Enjoy!

All the best,

The Global Grafx Crew
8/14/2014

Thus says the Lord: "Let not the wise man boast in his wisdom, let not the mighty man boast in his might, let not the rich man boast in his riches, but let him who boasts boast in this, that he understands and knows me, that I am the Lord who practices steadfast love, justice, and righteousness in the earth. For in these things I delight, declares the Lord.

- Jeremiah 9:23-24

And my God will supply every need of yours according to his riches in glory in Christ Jesus. - Philippians 4:19

_____
_____
_____
_____
_____
_____
_____
_____
_____
_____
_____
_____
_____
_____
_____
_____
_____

For by him all things were created, in heaven and on earth, visible and invisible, whether thrones or dominions or rulers or authorities—all things were created through him and for him. - Colossians 1:16

_____

_____

_____

_____

_____

_____

_____

_____

_____

_____

_____

_____

_____

_____

_____

_____

_____

_____

Because you have so little faith. Truly I tell you, if you have faith as small as a mustard seed, you can say to this mountain, 'Move from here to there,' and it will move. Nothing will be impossible for you." -- Matthew 17:20

_____

_____

_____

_____

_____

_____

_____

_____

_____

_____

_____

_____

_____

_____

_____

_____

_____

_____

So now faith, hope, and love abide, these three; but the greatest of these is love. -- 1 Corinthians 13:13

_____

_____

_____

_____

_____

_____

_____

_____

_____

_____

_____

_____

_____

_____

_____

_____

_____

_____

For there is a proper time and procedure for every matter, though a person may be weighed down by misery. - Ecclesiasties 8:6

_____
_____
_____
_____
_____
_____
_____
_____
_____
_____
_____
_____
_____
_____
_____
_____
_____
_____
_____

There is a time for everything, and a season for every activity under the heavens.
- Ecclesiasties 3:1

_____
_____
_____
_____
_____
_____
_____
_____
_____
_____
_____
_____
_____
_____
_____
_____
_____
_____

Every man shall give as he is able, according to the blessing of the Lord your God which he has given you.- Deuteronomy 16:17

_____
_____
_____
_____
_____
_____
_____
_____
_____
_____
_____
_____
_____
_____
_____
_____
_____
_____
_____
_____

Echo in my memory: "Humble yourselves, therefore, under the mighty hand of God so that at the proper time he may exalt you."
— 1 Peter 5:6

_____
_____
_____
_____
_____
_____
_____
_____
_____
_____
_____
_____
_____
_____
_____
_____
_____
_____

He gives power to the faint, and to him who has no might he increases strength. Even youths shall faint and be weary, and young men shall fall exhausted; but they who wait for the Lord shall renew their strength; they shall mount up with wings like eagles; they shall run and not be weary; they shall walk and not faint.

Jesus said, "Go home to your family, and report to them all that the Lord has done for you, and the mercy He has shown you."
- Mark 5

_____

_____

_____

_____

_____

_____

_____

_____

_____

_____

_____

_____

_____

_____

_____

_____

_____

_____

And my God will supply every need of yours according to his riches in glory in Christ Jesus. - Philippians 4:19

_____

_____

_____

_____

_____

_____

_____

_____

_____

_____

_____

_____

_____

_____

_____

_____

_____

_____

_____

_____

Love is patient and kind; love does not envy or boast; it is not arrogant or rude. It does not insist on its own way; it is not irritable or resentful; it does not rejoice at wrongdoing, but rejoices with the truth. Love bears all things, believes all things, hopes all things, endures all things. Love never ends.

1 Corinthians 13: 4-8

Man is destined to die once, and after that to face judgment. - Hebrews 9:27

Peace I leave with you, my peace I give unto you: not as the world giveth, give I unto you. Let not your heart be troubled, neither let it be afraid. – John 14:27

_____

_____

_____

_____

_____

_____

_____

_____

_____

_____

_____

_____

_____

_____

_____

_____

_____

_____

_____

Delight thyself also in the Lord: and he shall give thee the desires of thine heart.
- Psalm 37:4

_____

_____

_____

_____

_____

_____

_____

_____

_____

_____

_____

_____

_____

_____

_____

_____

_____

_____

Even in laughter the heart is sorrowful; and the end of that mirth is heaviness.
– Proverbs 14:13

_____

_____

_____

_____

_____

_____

_____

_____

_____

_____

_____

_____

_____

_____

_____

_____

Every good gift and every perfect gift is from above, and cometh down from the Father of lights, with whom is no variableness, neither shadow of turning. - James 1:17

_____
_____
_____
_____
_____
_____
_____
_____
_____
_____
_____
_____
_____
_____
_____
_____
_____
_____
_____
_____

Even in laughter the heart is sorrowful; and the end of that mirth is heaviness.
- Proverbs 14:13

_____
_____
_____
_____
_____
_____
_____
_____
_____
_____
_____
_____
_____
_____
_____
_____
_____
_____
_____
_____
_____
_____
_____

There hath no temptation taken you but such as is common to man: but God is faithful, who will not suffer you to be tempted above that ye are able; but will with the temptation also make a way to escape, that ye may be able to bear it.

- 1 Corinthians 10:13

Howbeit when he, the Spirit of truth, is come, he will guide you into all truth: for he shall not speak of himself; but whatsoever he shall hear, that shall he speak: and he will shew you things to come. - John 16:13

_____
_____
_____
_____
_____
_____
_____
_____
_____
_____
_____
_____
_____
_____
_____
_____
_____
_____
_____

And God said, Let us make man in our image, after our likeness: and let them have dominion over the fish of the sea, and over the fowl of the air, and over the cattle, and over all the earth, and over every creeping thing that creepeth upon the earth. - Genesis 1:26

Love is patient and kind; love does not envy or boast; it is not arrogant or rude. It does not insist on its own way; it is not irritable or resentful; it does not rejoice at wrongdoing, but rejoices with the truth. Love bears all things, believes all things, hopes all things, endures all things. Love never ends. - 1 Corinthians 13: 4-8

And above all things have fervent charity among yourselves: for charity shall cover the multitude of sins. Use hospitality one to another without grudging. As every man hath received the gift, even so minister the same one to another, as good stewards of the manifold grace of God. - 1 Peter 4:10

Global Grafx Press

823 Old Westtown Road
West Chester, Pennsylvania 19382

www.ingramcontent.com/pod-product-compliance
Lightning Source LLC
Chambersburg PA
CBHW041758040426

42447CB00001B/8